The town itself straddles the River Wye which is crossed by a famous medieval bridge still in use. Apart from the site being a natural one for a settlement (the Romans were here and an Iron Age fort was discovered on higher ground to the east at Ball Cross Farm), the existence of at least twelve wells of chalybeate-saturated water was another reason for its popularity. Most of these warm-water wells have been channelled underground into the Wye or have dried up, but they explain the name - *Bad kwell*, or *bathspring*.

It is almost certain that during the Roman occupation there was a village bath at the warm spring, here known as the Warm Well. The Roman altar found nearby and now to be seen at Haddon Hall shows a dedication to *Mars Braciaca* probably a Celtic god identified with the Roman deity associated with healing waters. The name may well be an attempt to spell out the Celtic *Brac* meaning free and *Iachau* meaning heal, i.e. free-healer, a tradition of healing confirmed by a medieval monk, William of Worcester, who described the River Wye which began at Buxton as the Holywell, as performing many miracles by making the sick well again. The name Holywell survives near the present recreation grounds.

In 1697, the 9th Earl of Rutland (afterwards 1st Duke), built a bath-house over the most famous of these wells, the Warm Well, and the building still stands in Bath Gardens. It contains the Duke's original stone bath but is not open to the public. The well itself was one of the two remaining to have a substantial flow of water above ground, though this is no longer the case. In 1817 it was restored and run with a reading room by the geologist White Watson.

The unique Derbyshire custom of well-dressing flourished here in the 1700s but lapsed only to be revived in 1971. Now as many as five wells are dressed here annually.

According to ancient chronicles Alfred the Great's son, Edward the Elder (reigned 901-924) ordered the building of a military post at Bakewell after he had succeeded in his campaigns against the Danish invaders. It is not known for certain where this was but it has been suggested that it was sited north east of Coombs Road near Riverdale Farm.

Opposite, clockwise from top left; the Vernon Chapel in the parish church, the Rutland Arms, the sign of 'The Old Original Pudding Shop', Portland Square, a distinctive old door front, bowls in Bath Gardens, a weir on the River Wye, children's paddling pool in the playground, a charming cottage and All Saints Church.

The idyllic river Wye north east of Bakewell

GW00725914

Over a century later in the reign of Edward the Confessor, the manor was Crown property. Subsequent Lords of the Manor included the Peverels, the Gernons and the Vernons of Haddon Hall. The last Vernon's co-heiress married into the Manners family (see page 13) and the Earls and Dukes of Rutland have held the lordship ever since.

The most outstanding feature of the town is the magnificent parish church of All Saints (see pages 8-10) which commands a dominant position on high ground to the west. Here are the memorials to the Vernons and Manners, though most to the latter lie in Bottesford Church in Leicestershire.

Standing in the centre of the town is the **RUTLAND ARMS**, a handsome Georgian coaching inn built to replace an older inn known as

The Rutland Arms Hotel

the White Horse which in the early 1800s had become inadequate to deal with the increase in coaching trade (as a result of turnpike road improvements from 1759 onwards), for the early years of the nineteenth century were the golden days of stage-coaches before the railways rapidly banished them, though stage-coaches and a horse-drawn char-a-banc were still to be seen in Bakewell before the Great War, albeit for the delectation of tourists rather than for normal commercial purposes. To the south (left) of the Rutland Arms, King Street passes westward to the **OLD TOWN HALL** where the King's justice used to be dispensed. The road turns and becomes South Church Street, passing the almshouses known as St

The Old Town Hall in King Street, built in 1709

North Church Street from the Churchyard

John's Almshouse and some attractive cottages on the right which had thatched roofs until a few years ago. After passing the former Vicarage and the old forge on the left, the road curves west towards Monyash and Leek.

To the north (right) of the church, North Church Street rises steeply past the churchyard, the Church and Chantry House where it turns and soon passes a turning to the Old House Museum (see page 11) and continues until it joins Stanedge Road where is situated S. Anselm's, a preparatory school for boys and girls.

Bagshaw Hall

Butter Cross

Bath Gardens

Bagshaw Hill leads east opposite the turning to the Old House Museum back into the town again and halfway down the hill is **BAGSHAW HALL** with the road continuing to descend into the town.

The old turnpike road, now the A6 Matlock-Buxton road, passes through the centre of Bakewell which means that it is at most times a very busy place. Bakewell has always been a bustling market town particularly on Mondays (Market Day) and on Saturday mornings.

The A6 north passes not far from the **BATH GARDENS** on the right and the Roman Catholic (formerly the Congregational) Church. The main building to be encountered on this road is the

St. John's Almshouses in South Church Street

The Town Hall

Sir Richard Arkwright developed the mills here further upstream using water power to carry on cotton-spinning, first started by him at Cromford. He built or converted several buildings in the town to house his workpeople.

In a cul-de-sac off the A6 near the Victoria Mill is the Milford House Hotel, a popular private hotel. Alongside is the stream with an attractive walk along its banks.

Due south from the town centre, the road leads straight out towards Haddon Hall keeping more or less parallel with the river, on the left bank of which is a public footpath. From the main road the towers and battlements can just be glimpsed tantalisingly through the trees. On the right, before Haddon is reached, there has been considerable modern development. Much of this is in the grounds of a former country house called Burton Closes which has the distinction of having been designed by Pugin in a spirited early Tudor style. It dates from 1847 and was once scheduled to be demolished. Luckily it was saved and is now an old people's home, though the park has been 'developed' and the whole area is now much changed.

Victoria Mill. A corn mill was recorded in Domesday Book and it may well have been on the site of this nineteenth century building. The huge iron mill-wheel now lies in the yard and can be seen from the road. It is sixteen feet in diameter and was providing power for grinding corn right up to the mid-1940s.

The Rutland Arms looks straight down into **RUTLAND SQUARE** which is the hub of present day Bakewell. The central feature is a fine war memorial cross combining the idea of Victory through Sacrifice of the lives of those from within a

The Old Market Hall, now the National Park Tourist Information Centre

The pack-horse bridge at Holme dating from 1664

radius of five miles of the cross who fell in the 1914-18 war. All the names appear in the porch of the former Bakewell and District War Memorial Cottage Hospital in Butts Road. The names of Bakewellians who fell in the last war are recorded on the base of the flag-staff in the Bath Gardens on which the Union Jack is flown on special occasions. The Square leads into Bridge Street, past the Old Market Hall. Before reaching the bridge, on the left, is Castle Street, a charming terrace of late Georgian houses. The bridge itself is early 14th century and though widened on the north side in the 19th century, it is none the less amazing to realise how well it copes with the ever-increasing flow of modern day traffic.

From the other side of the Wye can be seen the finest and most famous view of the town with the bridge in the foreground and the church spire a focal point in the distance. Here the road bifurcates twice, the North fork leading to Baslow and to the South, the B6048 ending at the old station yard industrial estate, golf course and showground and on to Chatsworth Park but is unsuitable for motor vehicles after the branch-off towards Pilsley. Between these two roads is Castle Hill at the base of which is Castle Hill House, built about 1700 and stuccoed in the 19th Century. It is now a boarding house for the Lady Manners School, founded in 1637 by Dorothy Vernon's daughter-in-law, Grace, as a grammar school and now part of the Comprehensive system, and standing in a prominent position on the west side of the town.

Leading off the Baslow Road half a mile further on is a lane leading to Holme, once a hamlet in its own right, but now part of Bakewell. Apart from some fine 18th century houses including Burre House, the home of local antiquarian, the late R. W. P. Cockerton and now the residence of Mr. Michael Cockerton, the main interest is in the very old **PACK-HORSE BRIDGE** and **HOLME HALL** a splendid country house built in the first year of the reign of King Charles I.

A market has been held in Bakewell from time immemorial and this custom was confirmed by royal charter in 1330. The stalls are set up behind the Old Market Hall, and although the market was once held every Friday, Monday is now Market Day.

Bridge Street

The modern Agricultural Centre

The Cattle Market is one of the largest in the county and plays an important part in the farming life of the area. It is not surprising how large a role agriculture plays in the life of the town, considering that it is in the heart of thousands of acres of arable and pastoral land. Neither is it surprising that one of Britain's best known agricultural shows is held here each year on the permanent showground to be found on the eastern boundary of the town on the east side of the river. The Bakewell Show is considered in more detail on page 14.

Bakewell has literary associations; in 1811 Jane Austen is said to have visited the town and stayed at the newly-built Rutland Arms. She used the town, lightly disguised, as 'Lambton' in *Pride and Prejudice*. The room she stayed in is still shown.

The Rev Francis Hodgson, Vicar and close personal friend of Lord Byron lived here, and John Taylor, the publisher of the poems of Keats and of John Clare, the Northamptonshire poet, was a frequent visitor to his brother James's house in King Street. Taylor was also editor of the *London Magazine* in the 1820s.

View of Rutland Square from Bath Gardens

Brief Notes on Some Historic Buildings

Probably the oldest house in Bakewell is **The Old House Museum**, in Cunningham Place off Church Street, and this merits special mention (see page 11).

Although **BAGSHAW HALL** presents a fine Carolean facade dating from 1684 when it was enlarged by one Thomas Bagshaw, it may well be as old as the Old House Museum as parts of the rear date from the early sixteenth century. It belonged to the FitzHerberts and for some years served as the town's Conservative Club, but it is once again a private residence.

The Old House Museum

The **Old Market Hall** is a prominent building in the centre dating from the early 17th century and was restored between the years 1968-71. It is now the National Park Tourist Information Centre, housing an exhibition and displays about the Town and National Park in general. It provides the latest information regarding services, events, accommodation, etc., and is open throughout the year except for Christmas.

In spite of dating only from 1709, the **OLD TOWN HALL** looks much older. In its time it has housed justices for the Quarter Sessions, and the bell to summon a fire-engine, and has been a working men's club, a school and is now an antique shop. Behind it are the **St. John's Almshouses** dating from the 17th century and opposite is **Catcliffe House**, an interesting mid-18th century house.

Bakewell Puddings

For millions who have never been near the town itself, the name Bakewell is familiar through the famous pudding. Its fame has gone round the world wherever the English language is spoken.

The story is said to have started at the White Horse Inn later the Rutland Arms where a Mrs Greaves would serve meals to coach passengers awaiting a change of horses. Below is an account which appeared in *The Derbyshire Countryside* some years ago.

'While Mrs Greaves was out of the kitchen one day, her assistant put the jam into the bottom of the pudding case (which was made of flaky pastry) and then put the filling on top. This particular dish should have had the jam on top, and the resulting pudding had a dark top and quite a different flavour. But the guests who ate it commented favourably on the new pudding, to Mrs Greaves' pleasure and her assistant's relief. The new recipe was carefully noted by Mrs Greaves and used thereafter for the making of Bakewell Puddings.'

'This dish is essentially a pudding, not a tart, and it should be eaten warm. In many parts of the country there are Bakewell tarts, so called, which have a big sale. But they are small things with much the same character as any other tart, except for the filling.'

Left: Bloomers Original Bakewell Pudding shop

The Old Original Bakewell Pudding shop

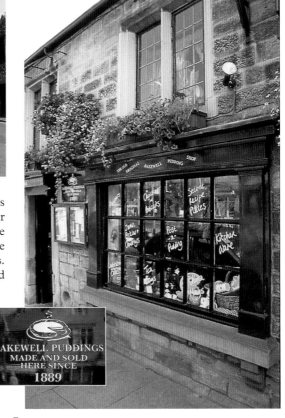

A Mr Radford now comes into the story. He was at one time a schoolmaster in Bakewell who later became an auctioneer. Like many men of his type and time, his education brought him many diverse tasks, one of which was the drawing up of wills. He drew up the will of Mrs Greaves's assistant and by it the original Bakewell Pudding recipe, in her own handwriting, passed to him. Already the pudding had become a national as well as a local favourite and the recipe was valued. Mr Radford passed the recipe to a Mr Bloomer so that he could make and sell the real thing. Now his descendants still bake the pudding according to the original recipe (which reposes in the firm's safe).

THE CHURCH OF ALL SAINTS

Anglo Saxon stones in the South Porch

The spire and unusual octagonal tower of Bakewell's exceptionally fine parish church are a landmark, and a focal point of Christian worship.

It is certain that there has been a Christian church on this site for over a thousand years though of the Saxon church practically nothing remains except a hint of Norman superimposed on Saxon work and a considerable collection of 9th and 10th century masonry and carved stones now mostly to be seen in the porch. There is an 8th century cross, the Great Cross, outside (believed to have come from a crossroads just north of the town) and part of another of the 10th century, brought here many years ago from Gladwin's Mark, Ashover.

Though there are traces of Norman work the bulk of the great church, as it now stands, dates from the 13th and 14th centuries with inevitable and considerable 19th century restoration. Luckily the work was carried out by the younger Gilbert Scott who was both thorough and highly sympathetic to the general characteristics of the church. Much had to be completely rebuilt, though one would hardly guess that today. The church is also fortunate in having a 1914-18 War Memorial side-altar and reredos designed by that distinguished 20th century architect, Sir Ninian Comper, who, with his son, also worked on the extensions to Derby Cathedral.

The massive nave was rebuilt in 1852 leaving only two Norman arches at the west end. It is easy to sneer at the Victorians, but the time will come when the merit of these often drastic restorations will be appreciated as it could be argued that the Victorians were among the greatest builders of all time. The nave of Bakewell Church is something of which any medieval builder could be proud.

Do not miss the monument to Sir Godfrey Foljambe and his wife in the South Aisle. Described by Sir Nikolaus Pevsner as *'an internationally remarkable monument'* it dates from about 1377 and is in alabaster with coats of arms above.

The south transept is famous for its Vernon Chapel (a Victorian reconstruction) with memorials to the Vernons and the Manners. Although most to the latter family lie in Bottesford

The 'internationally remarkable monument' to Sir Godfrey Foljambe and his wife, dating from around 1377

The Nave of All Saints Church

Monument to Sir John and Lady Manners (Dorothy Vernon)

Sir George Manners and his wife

The Vernon Chapel

Christ depicted in a section of the Nave's stained glass windows

Church, Leicestershire, there is a monument here to John Manners and his wife Dorothy Vernon and a splendid one to their son and successor, Sir George Manners, father of the 8th Earl of Rutland, and his wife Grace (née Pierrepont), who founded the Grammar School.

There are monuments to other members of the Vernon family, including the celebrated Sir George and his two wives. During the restoration and rebuilding in the last century, bones were discovered and were examined and identified as those of Dorothy Vernon before being reinterred.

Among the many other interesting things to note in the church are the carved choirstalls in the chancel and the late 13th or early 14th century sculptured font, with Our Lord in Glory on the west side and on His Right the Blessed Virgin Mary crowned as Queen of Heaven, followed by St Peter holding up the church, St Paul with the Sword of the Spirit, a Bishop (possibly St Chad), a priest holding a chalice, St John the Baptist and St John *'the beloved disciple'*- a fitting accoutrement to a church dedicated to All Saints.

One of the Museum's fascinating displays, and above, the charming exterior seen from Cunningham Place

THE OLD HOUSE MUSEUM

The Old House Museum is not only one of Bakewell's oldest and most interesting buildings, but also a triumph of what determined local people will do to preserve something worthwhile.

In the early '50s this building was a collection of shabby tenements with no modern amenities. Bakewell UDC issued a demolition notice and it seemed that another interesting old property was to disappear. In 1954 the Bakewell and District Historical Society was founded with the express purpose of saving the house. The executor of the last owner of the property presented it to the newly-formed Society and eventually the long task of restoring the building was begun.

The bulk of the present structure was built by Ralph Gell, of Hopton Hall near Wirksworth, in about 1534 possibly encasing an earlier timber-framed building. In appearance it resembled the usual type of yeoman's house of the period with limestone walls dressed with gritstone and with oak joists and rafters. The roof was hung with Derbyshire

A display of local marble ware

slate, pegged with oak. The core of this original house remains substantially the same in spite of considerable additions and alterations over the next three centuries. In about 1620 a new wing was built on to the north east end with mullioned windows and also a small porch.

Sir Richard Arkwright leased the building in 1778 and converted it to house some of his employees from the nearby Lumford cotton mill. He eventually sold out to the Duke of Devonshire who in turn sold it to the then master of Bakewell workhouse, a Mr Cunningham. The Arkwrights had made six dwellings; Cunningham lived in one and let the rest. For many years the building was known as Cunningham Place. By the time of the 1920s, a family called Harrison lived in part of the house which had no hot water system and an outside privy. In 1954 the executors of the last owner, Mr T. N. Harrison, presented the house to the Bakewell and District Historical Society who have cared for it ever since.

During the restoration work beams were discovered under ceiling boards, as were ancient windows and doorways and old stone fireplaces. Gradually the building revealed its secrets so that with this architectural knowledge plus the documentary evidence which has survived, an overall picture was pieced together to give a history of the house.

The Old House now houses a museum reflecting the various aspects of social life in Bakewell and Derbyshire in the past. It is also a centre for local historical research and a focal point of the Society's increasingly varied activities.

There are ten rooms to be seen and many interesting exhibits, all of which have been donated to the Museum.

SPORT AND RECREATION

Golf

There is a sporting little hilly nine-hole course near the old railway station with a club house and a resident steward. The Bakewell Golf Club was established in 1899 and has flourished ever since. Although on hilly ground and requiring an extra modicum of skill and determination, the course affords magnificent views over the Wye Valley and the surrounding countryside. No caddies are available but refreshments may be obtained in the club-house.

Hunting

The High Peak Harriers hunt the stone-wall country from Ashbourne to Buxton and from Chatsworth to Longnor. The hunt was started by a Mr Thornhill in 1848 from hounds belonging to the Marquess of Stafford. Past Masters have included Mr Nesfield who was one of the agents to the Dukes of Rutland, Colonel Robertson-Aikman (1901-1910) who brought his own hounds from Scotland, Lady Maud Baillie, a daughter of the 9th Duke of Devonshire, and the Misses May and Violet Wilson. At the time of writing the Senior Master is Mr M. Brocklehurst.

Hounds hunt mainly on Wednesdays and Saturdays and the kennels are at Shutts Lane, Bakewell. The Hunt holds point-to-point races and there is an annual hunt ball. Since 1920 the pack has been bred entirely as Stud Book Harriers and has featured prominently at Peterborough Hound Show.

Fishing

This part of the county has been made world famous for fishing by the works of Izaak Walton and his friend Charles Cotton. Although the Dove was their main fishing ground, the River Wye is in the same category and offers extremely good sport. That stretch of the river between Ashford Lake and Rowsley Bridge is part of the Haddon estate and

The Children's Playground

strictly private. It is mainly used for the benefit of the residents at the Peacock Hotel at Rowsley and the Rutland Arms, Bakewell, though the former hotel can supply 12 permits a day to the public for the Wye and two for the Derwent. The stretch between Ashford Lake and the Sheepwash at Ashford is also private and part of the Ashford Hall estate.

Other Activities

Cricket, football and tennis are played on the Rutland Recreation Ground situated between the River Wye and Haddon Road. In 1884 13 acres were opened for the purpose of public recreation. This land was actually conveyed to the Council in 1921 by the 8th Duke of Rutland and his son. Today there are hard tennis courts, cricket and football pitches, a putting green, a children's playground with a paddling pool and other facilities.

The Recreation Ground and Cricket Pavilion

Bakewell Cricket Club dates from 1861 and there is also a football club. The town's bowling green is in Bath Gardens. Bakewell is an important centre for walking and there is a fine range of footpaths and other routes including the Monsal Trail with access and parking at the old station. Details, maps etc. are available from the Tourist Information Centre in Bridge Street.

HADDON AND CHATSWORTH

Haddon Hall is closely linked to Bakewell, a mile or so to the south in a beautiful setting close to the river Wye. The Manners family, who inherited it from the Vernons, owned, as they still do, Belvoir Castle in Leicestershire and they preferred this to Haddon which they left but did not completely abandon, so that it lay sleeping and undisturbed for nearly two hundred years until the 9th Duke of Rutland gave it the kiss of life in the 1920s. He lovingly restored it over a period of years so that it is once again partially a family home.

The structure incorporates features from the 12th to the 16th centuries and the Banqueting Hall and Long Gallery are particularly fine. The myriad of diamond panes in the windows of the Long Gallery alternately billow in and out in an unusual fashion designed so as best to catch and diffuse the light and some of the small panes have names and dates scratched on them. They were etched in the 1920s by workmen who were engaged on the restoration and thus their names will survive for future generations of historians. George V and Queen Mary also signed their names on a wall in one of the rooms.

The best-known Vernon at Haddon was Sir George, known as '*The King of the Peak*', who lived in great style and is said to have been waited upon by eighty servants when entertaining in the Banqueting Hall. His daughter and co-heiress Dorothy married John Manners but the oft-told story of their romantic elopement has many elements of doubt. Sir George is not likely to have had any objections to marriage with a member of the illustrious Manners family and his great-grandson was eventually to become 8th Earl of Rutland. Although Sir George had another married daughter, he left Haddon in his will to Dorothy and her husband. The Manners crest is a peacock and this handsome bird can be seen carved in many places in the house and it also accounts for the name of several local public houses and hotels.

There could hardly be a greater contrast between the homely battlements of Haddon and the mighty grandeur of its neighbour Chatsworth. While Haddon is rugged, Chatsworth is classical Renaissance filled with works of art of the highest order. To see the House for the first time is an unforgettable experience; a perfect alliance between Man and the landscape. The waterworks here are the most elaborate of any private estate in Britain.

Bess of Hardwick's old house was replaced by her great-grandson the 1st Duke of Devonshire, who employed the architect Talman to build the present four-sided building. The 6th Duke in the nineteenth century added the north range of buildings ending in the Theatre Tower. It was the 6th Duke, too, who transformed the gardens at Chatsworth with the aid of his head gardener Joseph Paxton, who was to achieve fame in designing the Crystal Palace.

So much has been written about Chatsworth that it would be superfluous here to expound on the wonders to be seen both within and without. Although Chatsworth is a showplace visited by many thousands each year it is still at the same time the family home of the present Duke and Duchess of Devonshire.

Above left: The South Front of Haddon Hall

Chatsworth and the Michelangelo bridge

Hackney event

THE BAKEWELL SHOW

Every August sees one of the great days in Bakewell's calendar - the annual Bakewell Show. This has become one of the most celebrated agricultural shows in the country but its beginnings were fairly humble.

It all started in 1819, and was very much a local event. Until sometime in the 1920s it was financed and directed by the Dukes of Devonshire and Rutland and was mainly agricultural and horticultural.

Until the 1930s the Show was held on the recreation ground but then it acquired a permanent home in its present attractive position.

Apart from the stock exhibited - cattle, horses, sheep and goats, dogs are also shown as are poultry and pigeons. Show-jumping is an important part of the Show and the old shire horses, once on the wane, are now becoming an increasing attraction. Other notable parts of the proceedings are horticultural exhibits and agricultural machinery.

NEIGHBOURING BEAUTY SPOTS

Stanton Moor
To the south, on Stanton Moor, stands a folly tower erected in 1832 to celebrate the passing of the Reform Bill. Stanton Moor Edge belongs to the National Trust and is a marvellous vantage point for seeing the surrounding countryside. Not far from the tower is the prehistoric Nine Ladies stone circle, with the outlying stone known as The King's Stone. Public access is limited.

Lathkill Dale
Monyash, a small village to the west of Bakewell, is the beginning of Lathkill Dale. The River Lathkill is a trout stream meandering through fields and limestone outcrops, though it tends to dry up in summer. Charles Cotton thought it the purest

Lathkill Dale

water he had ever seen. Due south is Arbor Low, another ancient stone circle. The large stones are all now lying flat but if one can imagine them to be standing vertical, the comparison with Stonehenge would be obvious, for this is sometimes known as the Stonehenge of Derbyshire.

Monsal Dale

Monsal Dale

'. . . *now every fool in Buxton can be in Bakewell in half-an-hour and every fool in Bakewell at Buxton'.* These words are part of the famous attack made by John Ruskin upon the great railway bridge which straddles the Wye and carried the railway track over the dale. Although no longer serving its original purpose, it is now a vital part of the Monsal Trail.

The old rustic bridge sketched by Chantrey has long since been replaced by a metal substitute, but the old Bull's Head still stands on Headstone Head, though it is now renovated and known as the Monsal Head Hotel. From the Headstones a magnificent view of the Dale can be seen. The waterfall adds to the sounds as well as the sights in the landscape.

Ashford-in-the-Water

This close neighbour to Bakewell is one of Derbyshire's loveliest villages. The houses cluster close to the River Wye which is crossed by two old bridges, the most notable being the one over the

river near to the mill, a restored pack-horse bridge, and the sheep-wash bridge (closed to traffic), built in the 18th century as a turnpike bridge and until recently the sheep-wash below the bridge was in use. Ashford Hall, a fine eighteenth century house, was once the property of the Cavendishes but is now the home of the Olivier family one of whom was the late Lord Olivier, the distinguished actor.

At Ashford, well-dressing takes place on Trinity Sunday the day of the patronal festival of Ashford Church.

Millers Dale and Chee Dale

The name is a corruption of Millhouse Dale and there were once textile mills. Here are limestone cliffs, a hamlet called Millers Dale and the foundations of an ancient chapel in Monksdale.

Chee Dale is upstream and its 300 foot tor with the Wye gliding at its base is a wonderful sight.

To the north lie the most rugged parts of the Peak with Kinderscout and Bleaklow. There are also the famous Derwent and Ladybower reservoirs and Castleton, with its magnificent caves and bluejohn. To the west is Buxton, a fine eighteenth century town and to the south Dovedale and the Matlocks. Eastwards leads to industrial areas, but even here are places of interest such as Chesterfield's famous crooked-spired church.

Chee Dale

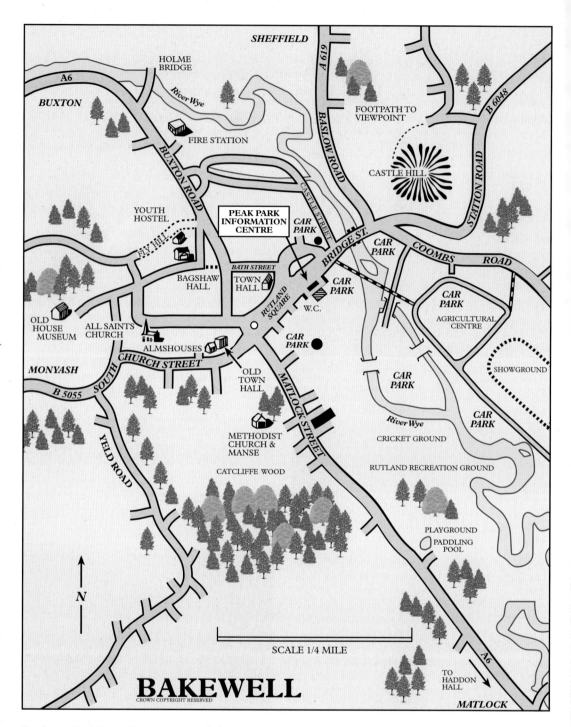

BAKEWELL

CROWN COPYRIGHT RESERVED

Based upon the Ordnance Survey mapping with the permission of The Controller of Her Majesty's Stationery Office.
© Crown copyright (399531)

Original text by Robert Innes-Smith.

Photographs by Gary Wallis, Nick McCann, Brian Lawrence and Peter Smith of Newbery Smith Photography.

Published by Derbyshire Countryside Ltd., Heritage House, Lodge Lane, Derby DE1 3HE. Tel 01332 347087. Printed in Great Britain.

ISBN 0 85100 114 9.

© Derbyshire Countryside Ltd. 2000.